GALAXY OF SUPERSTARS

Leonardo DiCaprio

Hanson

LeAnn Rimes

Spice Girls

Jonathan Taylor Thomas

Venus Williams

CHELSEA HOUSE PUBLISHERS

GALAXY OF SUPERSTARS

Venus Williams

Virginia Aronson

CHELSEA HOUSE PUBLISHERS
Philadelphia

Produced by
21st Century Publishing and Communications
a division of Tiger & Dragon International, Corp.
New York, New York
http://www.21cpc.com

Editor: Elaine Andrews
Picture Researcher: Hong Xiao
Electronic Composition and Production: Bill Kannar
Design and Art Direction: Irving S. Berman

CHELSEA HOUSE PUBLISHERS

Editor in Chief: Stephen Reginald
Managing Editor: James D. Gallagher
Production Manager: Pamela Loos
Art Director: Sara Davis
Director of Photography: Judy L. Hasday
Senior Production Editor: Lisa Chippendale
Publishing Coordinator: James McAvoy
Cover Illustration: Ian Varrassi/Brian Wible

Front Cover Photo: AP/Wide World Photos
Back Cover Photo: AP/Wide World Photos

The Chelsea House World Wide Web site address is
http://www.chelseahouse.com

First Printing

1 3 5 7 9 8 6 4 2

Library of Congress Cataloging-in-Publication Data

Aronson, Virginia.
  Venus Williams / Virginia Aronson.
  p. cm.—(Galaxy of superstars)
  Includes bibliographical references and index.
  Summary: A biography of the teenage tennis player who was ranked
in the top ten women players of the world in 1998.
  ISBN 0-7910-5153-6 (hardcover)
  1. Williams, Venus, 1980- —Juvenile literature. 2. Tennis players—
United States—Biography—Juvenile literature.
  [1. Williams, Venus, 1980-. 2. Tennis players. 3. Women—
Biography. 4. Afro-Americans—Biography.] I.Title II. Series.
GV994.W49A76 1999
796.342'092—dc21
  [B]   98-37650
                                                                 CIP
                                                                 AC

CONTENTS

1

TO BE THE BEST

"**S**ometimes people get on fire, and you have to be able to extinguish that no matter who they are," remarked an elated Venus Williams upon beating her 16-year-old Russian challenger, Anna Kournikova, to win the Lipton Championships women's tennis tournament on March 28, 1998, in Key Biscayne, Florida. "It's like the fifth biggest tournament, so I'm pretty happy about that," she said after the exciting event. "I was able to feel what it was like to win, and I think that will really help me, especially this year."

The year had already included the very first win in a professional singles championship tennis tournament for Venus, the spirited 17-year-old African American from Florida. At nearly six feet, two inches, Venus looks like a powerhouse, and she plays with patience and perseverance. "I just wasn't ready in the first set; it might as well have been someone else out there," admitted the forthright champ at Lipton. "But I slowly adjusted. I think that usually when people do lose, they beat themselves." In fact, the Russian teen, who had beaten four Top 10 players before losing to Venus, *had* committed more than 50

Venus Williams played her way to her first big win and the Lipton Championships trophy in March 1998 when she defeated Russia's Anna Kournikova in the women's final match.

"bloopers" (unforced errors) in a match undermined by peer pressure, an unavoidable fact of life for most teenagers all over the world.

In accepting the crown, Venus became the first American-born woman to win the Lipton Championships since Chris Evert's victory in 1986. Venus simultaneously advanced her rapid rise in the rankings, moving into the No. 10 slot. "I'm coming," warned the long-legged teen with the colorful beaded braids. "Don't rush me."

Williams, who hands out the plastic beads from her hair to tennis fans between matches, has been credited with arousing new interest in the sport, especially among young people. "Venus is the best thing that has happened to American tennis in a long time," states Harry Marmion, president of the U.S. Tennis Association. NBC's tennis commentator Bud Collins agrees: "Venus is a godsend. She's calling attention to the game, and the game needs that now. She's the Tiger Woods of tennis."

"I hope so," Venus has responded. Often compared to the young golf icon, another sports superstar who is African American (Woods is also of Thai and Native American descent), Venus candidly acknowledges their similarities, stating, "He's different from the mainstream, and in tennis I also am. I'm tall. I'm black. Everything's different about me. Just face the facts."

Venus also must respond to constant public comparisons to her younger sister, Serena. At 16, Serena has, like her sister, moved up dramatically in the world tennis rankings, sometimes meeting with Venus in professional matches. Also like her sister, Serena fascinates fans with her stunning serves and powerful

Venus displays her power-house style as she returns a serve at the U.S. Open in August 1997. Although she lost in the finals to defending champion Martina Hingis of Switzerland, Venus jumped from 66th to 26th in women's rankings.

return hits as hundreds of bright beads bounce in her hair. In 1997's Ameritech Cup, held in Chicago, Serena beat the world's fifth-ranked player, veteran tennis pro Mary Pierce, as well as the popular Monica Seles, who had won 41 previous professional tennis events. Serena's world ranking lept from 304th to 100th. "I think I've emerged," she has said.

Despite her sister's rising talent and popularity, Venus is confident that *she* will one day be the best women's tennis player in the world. In fact, she wears a necklace made from dice that spell out "Venus #1." She tells the press, "I don't think it's possible that I won't be Number One."

Venus Williams is not being egotistical in making such a grand statement about her own future. She is not full of hot air either. Rather, this type of admission illustrates quite well the special way this teen tennis phenom has been coached to look at herself. As a young African-American woman raised in the projects in Compton, California, a gang-infested area of South Los Angeles, who practiced tennis on glass-strewn municipal courts, a too-tall girl with braces on her teeth, a black person playing what has typically been a white upper-class sport, *Venus Williams sees herself as a winner.* And she is willing to do what it takes and to make the required sacrifices in order to fulfill her own potential. "I'm sure I'll get where I want to go," shares the gifted girl with the wide grin. "My parents taught us to believe in ourselves, to have confidence. I can't remember a time I didn't feel good about myself."

Venus Williams was ranked No. 5 as of August 1998, clearly one of the world's best tennis players. Her blistering serve has been clocked at more than 120 mph. She is an all-court player with a superstrong backhand and a graceful forehand stroke, and she is *fast*. She has played remarkably well in tournaments in this country and others, earning hundreds of thousands of dollars in a single afternoon. By the age of 15, Venus had scored a $12 million multiyear endorsement deal to represent the sportswear company Reebok. Before she had graduated from a Palm Beach area high school—early, at the age of 16—Venus Williams was already an internationally known tennis player, a millionaire, a teen idol, a fashion icon, and a celebrity sports figure. While her peers were concerning themselves with dates, the prom, and yearbook pictures, Venus was busy scheduling tournaments in France and Italy, speaking to the international press, and posing for photographs that appear in newspapers and magazines all over the world.

How does someone this young handle so much pressure—on the court, and off? Venus Williams relies on the love and support of her close-knit family, her faith in God, and her ability to focus on her goals. She works hard at being a winner, and she enjoys it: "A lot of people have more problems than going out and being the best. A lot of people are unhappy working nine to five, struggling, doing all kinds of things to keep afloat. I don't look at the practice and discipline as pressure; I look at it as working to be the best. I shouldn't want it to come easy, because that way it isn't a challenge."

The life of Venus Williams has not been an easy or problem-free ladder to the top. In fact, if it were not for the incredible foresight and strong guidance of a self-proclaimed "little ignorant man out of southeast Compton"—her father and mentor, Richard Williams—Venus would not be who she is today, a gutsy teen headed for greatness, heralded by many as the future of women's tennis. "When Venus is nineteen, her average serve is going to be 130 miles an hour," Richard predicts. "When Venus is twenty? And her whole body fills in? And she's playing serve-and-volley? Boy, I'm going to feel sorry for those other girls."

Richard Williams may be exaggerating a bit, but people are taking him—and his superstar daughter—*very* seriously.

Venus's smashing two-handed drive was not enough to give her a victory at her second Wimbledon competition in July 1998, when she lost the quarterfinal match to Jana Novotna of the Czech Republic. At 18, however, Venus's dreams of a Wimbledon trophy are far from over.

2

HARD BEGINNINGS

Venus Williams's first and current coach, long-time manager, and biggest fan is her father, Richard Williams. But when Richard was young and an athlete himself, he avoided tennis, which he saw as "a sissy game." He played basketball, football, and golf while working a number of jobs, a boy from the "poorest family" in the "poorest section" of Shreveport, Louisiana.

One of five children, Richard was the only son of Julia Williams, a single mother who had to support her family by picking cotton. She died in 1985. "My mother was my dad, my psychiatrist, my hero, the greatest person who ever lived," Richards says now. "She taught me pride, decency, religion, and that civilization would disappear when the family went bad." As a boy, Richard accompanied his mother to the fields where she labored. When she asked him afterward if he would want to work that hard all his life, the message, Richard says, was "Get an education and then you will never have to work [that] hard."

After high school, Richard moved to Chicago and worked in construction. When he was 20 years old, he moved to the Watts section of Los Angeles, where he

Dubbed the "Cinderella of the Ghetto," Venus began playing tennis at the age of four, practicing on the dangerous, litter-strewn public courts of the projects. From the first, she showed the heart and determination of the champion she is today.

formed his own security business, Samson Security. He fell for and married a nurse he met in church, Oracene Price. The couple had five daughters: Yetunde, Isha, and Lyndrea, followed by Venus Ebone Starr Williams on June 17, 1980, and Serena 15 months later.

After watching the winner of a televised tennis match accept a check for thousands of dollars, Richard decided to groom his two youngest girls to be tennis champions. A self-taught player, he also had started the older girls in the sport and reports that, "Yetunde was very good. Isha was awesome. Lyndrea too. Serena might be the best. But Venus was a champion the first day." Venus's father explains, "A champion has four qualities: they're rough, they're tough, they're strong, and they're mentally sound—she is all that." According to Richard, all of his girls showed talent, but only Venus and Serena fell in love with the sport. As a six-year-old, Venus says, "I thought I was going to be Number One."

Venus actually began playing tennis when she was only four. Serena began the following year. The family lived in Compton, California, a ghetto known for its gang violence, where the only tennis courts the girls could use were the free public courts covered with graffiti and located in gang territory. Richard now describes Compton as a city where "AK-47s, drugs, PCP, ice, and welfare checks are more prevalent than anywhere else in the world." He has written about this time in their lives: "Venus and Serena were shot at by the gang members [the Bloods] while practicing tennis, and they [the girls] hit the ground. Mr. Williams

Venus is always comfortable being in the limelight. Here, at 15, she chats with the media during a tennis clinic for underprivileged young people in Los Angeles. She had already turned pro and was well known as a former star on the junior tennis circuit.

was beaten up several times. . . . After about seven months, he had earned their respect."

Richard still tells stories about the girls' early years of practice with their near misses on dangerous turf, about how the gang members he had won over guarded the grounds while his kids hit tennis balls on cracked courts pock-marked from drive-by shootings. But he also recalls Venus's immediate determination and pure joy. If he brought 550 balls to the unkempt public tennis courts, the four-year-old would want to hit all of them, at first averaging four or five over the worn net. One day she hit a thousand balls, then asked for more. He began to call her "Cinderella of the ghetto."

On Their Own Turf

The U.S. Tennis Association has never attempted to develop the game of tennis in the inner city. Perhaps this is one of the reasons why the sport is currently on the decline in

America. "It's pretty sad," admits U.S.-born female tennis player Lindsay Davenport. "People in our country aren't playing right now, and they're not watching too much either." U.S. Tennis Association president Harry Marmion admits to the current dearth of American tennis talent, but asserts, "This is a serious problem, and I'm determined that we're going to solve it."

Yet no U.S. tennis champion—male or female—has *ever* emerged from a national program, including the association's $3.6 million player-development program. The history of women's championship tennis players is full of stories of young girls who rose to prominence under the tutelage of their own fathers, a number of whom were self-taught tennis coaches like Richard Williams. But unlike the Cinderella story of Venus Williams, tennis champions have rarely emerged from the ghetto. Historically, tennis has been a sport mainly for the wealthy.

Originally created in France in 1427, "court tennis" was a social event and garden-party game for ladies and gentlemen of old money and upper social class standing. Right from the start, tennis was a game for women, too. The early female players wore ground-length skirts, petticoats, corsets, and collars up to their chins. Some managed to master the game and took it seriously enough to become our earliest tennis aces. But women were not allowed to compete—and perspire—in public for many years.

By 1874, "lawn tennis," as it was then called, had spread from the British Empire to America and, in 1884, the All England Croquet and Lawn Tennis Club in Wimbledon adopted a ladies' championship. First prize was a silver flower basket, second prize a silver mirror and hairbrush. Three years later, America held its first championship event for women. Public courts had begun to appear throughout the country, but the game remained a social event for upper-class women and men.

After World War I, French champion Suzanne Lengler revolutionized women's tennis by sporting shorter tennis skirts (to the mid-calf), outfits designed by a French couturier worn without a corset underneath. She also set new standards for athleticism and training.

The women players who followed Lengler copied her fashions, improved their tennis, and brought color and allure to the game. Many continued to protest the inequities of a sport still generally regarded as a rich white man's game.

Considered by many to be the foremost woman tennis player of her time, American Helen Wills (left) shakes hands with her opponent after retaining her title at Wimbledon. Between 1923 and 1938, Wills won the U.S. singles title seven times and the British singles title eight times.

A Long Road

After World War II, women tennis players were different. They were more independent, often marrying late and holding jobs, and they wore practical, functional tennis outfits and sneaker-style tennis shoes. They learned to play more aggressively but were soon outshone by the most publicized player of the era, Gertrude "Gorgeous Gussy" Moran. When Gorgeous Gussy played at Wimbledon in 1949, she wore panties trimmed with lace under her short tennis skirt, an act of defiance that helped to bring the public spotlight to women's tennis for the next decade.

During the first half of the century, the United States Lawn Tennis Association (USLTA) admitted no black members. In fact, most of the private clubs where matches were played barred entry to all people of color. Black tennis players formed their own national organization in 1916, the American Tennis Association. In 1948, Dr. Reginald Weir became the first African American to play in a USLTA tournament. In 1949, superstar Althea Gibson became the first black woman to play in the all-white tournament championships.

In 1968, the game of tennis changed even more by opening the major championships to professionals as well as amateurs. "Open tennis" meant that players who "turned pro" competed for prize money, an incentive that drew many more players to the game. Once players could make a living at the sport, tennis was no longer a country-club game solely for the social elite.

Women, however, still battled for equal pay and equal recognition. Men owned, operated, and promoted all tennis tournaments, and their cash prizes were double, triple, even as much as 12 times the amount awarded to the women champions. Finally, the female tennis pros of the 1970s proved their equality on the courts when female tennis champion Billie Jean King beat Bobby Riggs, a male player who had publicly insulted women in the sport. "The Battle of the Sexes" was played in the Houston Astrodome in 1973, before a crowd of 30,000. It was, at the time, the biggest match in the history of tennis, capturing an estimated 50 million television viewers, many seeing the game for the first time. When King took home the trophy—and $300,000 in prize money and endorsements—viewers began to flock to the newly established women's tennis tour, the Virginia Slims Invitational.

By this time, the sport was more than 100

In 1957, Althea Gibson, here with her gold plate trophy, became the first African American to win a Wimbledon championship and, in 1958, to go on to the finals of the U.S. Open. Thirty-nine years later, Venus Williams became the first black woman since Gibson to reach the U.S. Open finals.

years old and, for the first time, the game attracted thousands of spectators and participants, not just wealthy white men in private, exclusive country clubs. Tennis had evolved into an inclusive, all-American game, open to players of all ages and nationalities and both sexes. It still helped if you were a rich white male athlete, but it was possible to become a tennis champion even if you were a poor black girl out of the Compton projects.

Venus Rising

Before she had even won a tournament, Venus Williams was already a star. Many tennis fans knew about the gifted young tennis player before she was 12 years old because she had appeared in *Sports Illustrated,* on national television, and on the front page of *The New York Times.* But her father was very careful about Venus's media appearances, and he limited the junior events she signed up for. He protected his daughter from the beginning of her career—and with ample reason. Too many young athletes burn out, with serious physical injuries and an overload of emotional stress, ruining forever their enjoyment of the sport and missing out on or totally destroying their childhoods. Too many young tennis stars in the making have suffered, typically at the hands of, and/or for the love of, their parents.

"We planned careers for our kids before they were born," Richard told a television correspondent in Los Angeles when Venus was a junior player. "Most parents say, 'I support what my kid wants to do.' But no kid knows what he wants to do. It's up to the parents to decide." Richard and Oracene believed that it was up to the parents of young tennis players to limit their children's exposure as well, but they could not deny their tennis-loving daughter the opportunity to continue playing the sport—as long as she stayed in school. "If it was up to me, she wouldn't be out on that court for another nine years. I would like to see her get an education," Richard told a sportswriter when Venus was a junior tennis ace. "There's too many kids out there that are nothing but kids and they should be in school. . . .

[I]f you don't have education, you don't have anything. You can have all the money in the world, but you need an education."

In addition to criticizing the common practice of letting kids drop out of school to pursue tennis careers, Richard Williams protested against parents who pushed their young kids out into the limelight for the purpose of worldwide fame and fortune. He explained to the press in 1991 that he saw this as a selfish choice for the parents of preteen athletes like Venus: "So many people say you're stupid if you don't do this and you don't do that. You just have to have your own values and your goals and do not detour from it. . . . There's nothing wrong with having a million dollars. I'm not saying I want to be poor. I'm tired of being poor. But I feel like as long as you have the love of your kids, you couldn't be poor. You have something that's really great. And it's not the kids [that] want a million dollars, the kids just want love. The parents have learned what money can do and what you can have. And I think that when you start prostituting your kid that way, you're not a good parent."

Richard kept Venus—and later, Serena—away from full-time involvement in what he saw as a cutthroat kiddie circuit full of horrible-acting parents and children who hated what their parents were forcing them to do. He also kept Venus in school and refused to rely on a sports-management company to run his daughter's career. "A lot of people tell me that the younger they are when they go out there, the more money you get. . . . I would rather see her out there when she's twenty years old. By that time she would have had four years of college.

As a U.S. Open runner-up, Venus appears on The Montel Williams Show *in 1997 with her father and coach, Richard (left). As coach and father, Richard has watched carefully over his daughter's career, encouraging her to be a champion but seeing to it that she never neglects her education.*

There's too many kids out there now not able to talk, they can't speak correctly, they can't make decisions. The agent makes the decisions, the parents are making the decisions, television's making their decisions, newspapers are making their decisions. The kid is just something out there like a piece of meat."

Richard Williams made the decisions himself for his family, including choices none of the other tennis players' parents were making. He took away Venus's tennis racket for a year when she was five, for example, "because she loved it too much. I wasn't looking to develop a tennis player, I was looking to develop a human being," he says now. Richard employed such an uncommon training method mainly to help his child keep tennis in perspective. While she was a preteen, Richard limited her practice time to two-and-a-half hours, three times a week, instead of the usual six or seven hours a day, six days a week. "Sure, I could have a superstar at fourteen. And I'm going to have nothing but a problem at twenty-two," he explained.

So, unlike the majority of the girls she was beating on the tennis court, Venus Williams was experiencing a rather normal childhood. Ignoring all of the critics who claimed that Richard Williams's atypical training choices slowed his daughter's development as a tennis player, Venus's father did not detour from the family's values and goals. Venus went to school, practiced her tennis regularly but not daily, and limited her matches in the junior tennis circuit, which requires extensive traveling during the school year. "She needs time to get her education," Richard declared, "because all these girls who come along chewing gum and not being able to speak that well, what happens to them when their [tennis] careers are over?" And, despite all of her father's critics' protests, Venus Williams excelled at the game, winning virtually every junior event she entered. At age 10, she won the southern California girls' 12-and-under title. And her star just kept on rising.

3

FAMILY, FAITH, AND FOCUS

"In 1991, I was eleven and four months when my family moved to Florida so I could get better training," Venus Williams recounts. "I used to play with my dad, but then I got too good for him." No longer the "normal kid" who played superior tennis on inferior courts, as a preteen Venus became a tennis star in training. She began attending the International Tennis Academy at the Grenelefe Resort near Orlando, where she was in the professional program offered to players aged 10 to 18 by tennis instructor Rick Macci.

Macci's tennis camp accommodated up to 40 young players who paid $2,200 per month each for room, board, tennis instruction, and transportation to and from the local schools. Because she was so gifted, Venus attended free of charge. Macci became her coach, a position he retained until 1995.

"I could see a Michael Jordan-type quality to her even then," Coach Macci recalls about the lanky girl player he had scouted when she was only 10. At Richard Williams's invitation, Macci had flown out to Compton to watch Venus (and Serena) play. Richard drove the tennis coach

---

Years of discipline and hard work culminated in Venus's victory in the Lipton Championships when she became the first American-born woman to win in 12 years.

to East Rancho Dominguez Park in a dented Volkswagen bus filled with discarded clothes and rolling tennis balls. Carefully ignoring the bums and drug addicts who were passed out all over the grass courtside, Macci observed the powerful Williams girls. He was especially awed by Venus, who left the courts to use the bathroom by walking on her hands, punctuating her trip with backward cartwheels! Struck by what a "tremendous natural athlete she was," Macci offered Venus a scholarship to his training facility.

The Williams family relocated, eventually settling in Delray Beach, a lovely coastal town in south Florida. Venus attended Carver Middle School while training intensely with Coach Macci.

Unbeaten on the junior circuit (63-0), Venus quit playing the children's tournaments in 1991. At her father's bidding, she did not play another tournament match for three years. "I might be doing it the wrong way," Richard Williams stated frankly, "but in the end she will benefit from it." Both Richard and Oracene believed that too much competitive tennis too early in life would hamper Venus's ability to learn and experiment on the court, while also distracting her from her education and growing-up process off the court.

No tennis player, male or female, had achieved superstar championship stature without refining their game in the junior circuit. The experts wondered: Could the 11-year-old tennis prodigy adequately develop her skills while playing in relative isolation, without facing the special pressures tournament competition provides? Young Venus began to serve as an experiment in the world of professional tennis: Was the junior circuit with all of its intensive competition *really* necessary in breeding a champion? "I think I can change the game," Venus announced.

Under Macci's wing, however, Venus practiced as long and hard as the rest of the kids who took their tennis seriously. "Six hours a day, six days a week for four years," remembers Macci. "There wasn't a day that the girl would not hit two hundred serves." All of the Tennis Academy children worked hard. Macci admitted, "You hate to use the word 'job' in connection with a kid, but if they want to get good, they've got to put in the work."

Getting Good

Starting in the 1970s and following in the footsteps of American favorite Chris Evert, a long line of precocious teenage tennis sensations have "put in the work" early, and some of these kids certainly *did* "get good." Playing in her first tournament at age eight, "Chrissie" Evert was ranked No. 1 in the world by the time she was 20. Famous, well-paid, and attractive, Evert's success lured thousands of young girls into the game, spawning a generation of teenage tennis players with braces on their teeth and braids in their hair. Some of the most famous and most youthful girls who have reigned supreme on the professional tennis circuit include Tracy Austin, Monica Seles, Jennifer Capriati, Steffi Graf, Mary Pierce, Gabriele Sabatini, Pam Shriver, and Andrea Jaeger.

Pro tennis can be a positive experience for young women, offering girls the opportunity to stretch their limits, fulfill their potentials, obtain financial independence, travel widely,

Showing the strain of being a child tennis star, a dispirited, 17-year-old Tracy Austin lost in the semifinals at Wimbledon in 1980. Pushed to the utmost, young players like Tracy often burn out before they are 20.

and have some fun. But as Richard Williams has pointed out, the risks are big and too many girls end up paying with permanently injured bodies, scarred psyches, lost opportunities, and missed childhoods.

When Tracy Austin first appeared at Wimbledon in 1977, she weighed 95 pounds and dressed in pinafores. Two years later at age 16, she became the youngest female to win a U.S. singles championship. "They said my mom tried to make me look like a little girl," Tracy stated as an adult. "But I *was* a little girl. I didn't mature quickly, physically or emotionally. . . . I think anybody going through adolescence has a tough time among their peers. And here I was growing up in front of the public, in front of the press, and the press was saying things that weren't true."

Like most of the child stars of the time, Tracy Austin suffered injuries that ruined her career. The injuries were the result of improper training, the physical vulnerability of a growing child, and the unrelenting intensity of the professional tennis circuit. Tracy says now, "I think many young players have learned and benefited from what happened to me, but they have also been hurt by the fact that I won the U.S. Open at sixteen. I think I started a belief that one *could* win the U.S. Open at sixteen, and therefore people started to put a lot of pressure on young players. . . . If a seventeen-year-old girl is only thirteenth in the world, the parents, the press, the agents, and the players start asking, 'What's taking you so long?'"

Monica Seles was embroiled in a well-publicized controversy from the early start of her career, when she was the youngest female to win the French Open and the Australian Open, two of the most important professional tennis events. "It always seems," she said at 17, when she was the youngest No. 1 player in history, "that when people talk about me, they invent mean things. In the beginning I thought it would be a miracle to become the best, but today I cry about it."

The average age of the world's Top 10 women tennis players steadily rose from not quite 23 in 1962 to 27 in 1971. By 1991, however, the average age of the world's 10 best women had plummeted to 20. In 1998, there were six teenage girls who ranked among the top 30 tennis players in the world.

Girls who play on the professional tennis circuit find to their dismay that they tend to age quickly. The sun prematurely wrinkles their skin, the isolation and extreme pressure to perform professionally—on and off the court—inevitably leads to growing up fast, too fast. Yet, they often fail to mature normally. They miss out on school, socialization with peers of both sexes, and the time to "hang out" and just be a kid. Sometimes all they know is tennis. As a sportswriter once explained, "Most kids develop. They read books, they meet new people, they have new experiences. But kids in tennis keep doing the same things. Nothing new happens to them, so they have nothing to say."

Plenty to Say

"Education is more important than tennis right now," Venus Williams once told *Seventeen* magazine. "Whatever I put into my head will stay there forever, and that's not necessarily true of tennis. Science is my favorite subject.

Can you believe that in 1923 explorers found a prehistoric fish off the coast of Madagascar that was supposed to be extinct, like, five hundred million years ago? Learning about that stuff is so cool."

Richard Williams took Venus out of the public junior high she was attending at age 13 in favor of home schooling by her family (one of her older sisters now studies medicine, the other law) and a number of tutors. She then enrolled in a private school, where she excelled. At 14, Venus was enthralled with paleontology, the study of prehistoric life forms, because she liked "digging into the past. Maybe because I wasn't there." Her education included speaking to children at inner-city schools. "I know I should go back there," Venus said, "because that's where I'm from. It's my roots."

"They say Jennifer's [Capriati] father was a fool," Richard Williams candidly stated to *The New York Times Magazine.* He was referring to the talented young tennis champ's early pro status at age 13, and her later, very public problem with drugs. "She was a great kid at fourteen. At fifteen, she lost her smile. At sixteen, there were problems. What happened? I want to make sure that doesn't happen to my kids," Richard worried.

His worries were not unfounded. By the time Venus was 14, she was begging her parents to allow her to turn pro. In response to Jennifer Capriati's arrest for drug possession in 1994, Venus had told *Sports Illustrated for Kids,* "Now I think I should take my time and be a child as long as I can." But this attitude did not last long, and Venus, who was already six-feet tall, soon resumed her pleading. The Williams family

finally voted on whether or not Venus should turn pro, with Richard abstaining. The votes came in: It was time for Venus to turn professional, to play against the best tennis aces in the women's tournaments—with world rankings, international press, lots of prize money, and the accompanying physical stress and psychological pressure.

"I opposed her decision," Richard revealed later, "but she went on and made that decision in spite of what I said. . . . I admire her for standing up for what she believes." Oracene also tried to talk Venus out of the early career choice but finally gave in to her determined

Her family provides a strong foundation for Venus, here getting a loving pat from her mother, Oracene. As a close-knit family, they depend on one another for encouragement and support.

"My mom braids them, and I bead them," says Venus of her trademark cornrows. Here, she toys with her beads as she contemplates her game during an interview in Oakland, California.

daughter. "I'm not that worried about it now," her mother said once her daughter had turned pro. "I can't control her destiny. It's up to her." As long as she maintained her A average in school, the Williamses allowed Venus to play pro tennis.

In October 1994, Richard took the family to Busch Gardens, a fun-filled theme park in Tampa, Florida. After a great vacation, Venus made her professional debut at the Bank of the West Classic in Oakland, California, where she amply demonstrated her raw talent and impressed the media. "I like answering questions. I think it's fun," the charming teen told the crush of reporters.

Venus became a professional tennis player

at the tender age of 14—just before the Women's Tennis Association (WTA) ruled that to prevent Capriati-like burn-out, players under 18 were to be restricted in the number of tournaments they could play. The following year, Richard threatened to sue the WTA if it ever refused to let 14-year-old Serena compete in a pro tournament.

With *two* pro teens under his roof, Richard had twice the worries but, it turns out, was still able to provide more than adequate guidance. According to Coach Macci, "Richard always wants to be in control, and that's not bad. He has done what he thought in his heart was best for his girls. He gets an A-triple plus for being the type of parent he is. He's got educated, well-mannered kids who have their priorities in line."

Like their older sisters, Venus and Serena have been raised in Richard and Oracene's faith: the family are all devout Jehovah's Witnesses, who do not drink, smoke, gamble, or do drugs. While growing up in California, the girls accompanied the rest of the family to preach door to door, and they attended Kingdom Hall to worship three times a week. In keeping with their faith, birthdays are not observed.

The Williamses are disciplined people, and the family rules are strictly observed. Venus and Serena are not allowed to date; they do their homework and speak politely. Television is limited to no more than two hours per week, and parties are off limits. The girls are not allowed to clap at tennis matches.

To protect his girls from physical injury, Richard put a cap on the number of professional tournaments he allowed both of his young daughters to play in each year. The year she

Confident in her ability to become a tennis superstar, Venus still has no trouble being a fun-loving teenager as she shows off her talent in playing air guitar with her racket.

was 15, for example, Venus could only play in five pro tournaments, while most pros play an average of 14. So Venus knew that she would not be pushed into overdoing it. "I like that I have an exact time to go to school and do my homework," she stated at the time. Her life remained secure in its routine and semblance of normalcy.

Not Poor Anymore

Financially, however, things changed dramatically for the Williams family once Venus turned pro. Although she was not winning any tournaments or earning any fat purses, in 1995

Venus had signed the multimillion-dollar endorsement deal with Reebok. Richard Williams also received a consultant's salary from the company, and the family soon moved to Palm Beach Gardens, a sprawling 10-acre estate near West Palm Beach, Florida. Here the girls could practice on their own tennis courts.

As a spokesmodel for Reebok, Venus began wearing the company's newest tennis outfits and footwear while competing in pro events. She also agreed to provide feedback on the various styles she was modeling for them. Venus talked to *Seventeen* magazine about the new tennis clothing line manufactured by Reebok called (you guessed it) The Venus Williams Collection: "The things I like are the denim skirts and dresses. They're cool," Venus gushed.

When Reebok signed up the enthusiastic 14-year-old athlete, she had not won a tournament since she was 10. But the savvy sportswear company predicted— correctly—that Venus Williams was headed for superstardom and would prove to be a highly visible model for their sports-clothes product line. Reebok was betting on Venus to revitalize a stagnating game whose base was older, predominantly white fans. The vice president of Reebok's women's footwear line announced, "She's the future." Venus's pleased father half-joked, "I don't know anyone who's done what Venus did. She should go right to the Hall of Fame. She's going to be there anyway, so why waste time?"

4

"I CAN DO THIS. I KNOW I CAN."

In 1997 the *Miami Herald* ran a story naming all of the celebrities who would participate in an upcoming charity walk to benefit female athletes. Venus Williams was listed after Martina Navratilova, possibly the best female tennis player in history. (In the 1990s, Navratilova held the world record for winning streaks in singles *and* doubles; that is, beating all challengers, both on her own and with a partner.) Venus was 16 years old and had not won even one pro tournament . . . yet.

Richard Williams had returned to his role of tennis coach in 1995, utilizing a unique style rich with encouragement and praise. From the shade beside the tennis court where his daughters practiced their game, Richard would call out, "Way to move, Venus! That's why you're going to be a superstar." If Venus hit the ball into the net, her father would yell, "That's all right, Venus. That was a great shot." When Venus ran over to kiss him during a break, Richard would say, "You're a great kid, Venus." When she said, "I love you, Daddy," he would rejoin, "I love you, too, Venus Williams."

At the Evert Cup in March 1997, Venus shows the aggressive style that catapulted her from the 211th ranking to the 27th by the end of the year.

At her U.S. Open debut in 1997, Venus began toning down her smashing serves and mixing her shots to play a more full-court game. She won match after match against top-ranked women to reach the finals.

To discourage Venus from putting herself under excessive pressure to win, Richard devised an unusual system. "Every time she loses, I pay her fifty dollars," he claimed. "Venus says she has more fifty-dollar bills than she knows what to do with."

Without the pressure to excel—from either her family or her coach-father—Venus was able to enjoy her daily practice and enter her early tournaments with confidence and a joyful anticipation. She practiced four hours a day, six days a week. (Her private school allowed her to leave at 12:30.) She typically practiced hitting the ball with men, tennis pros who serve the ball harder and faster than their female counterparts. Whenever she lost her matches, Richard eased her disappointment with kindness, making up excuses for her and continuing to reassure his daughter that she was a surefire No. 1 champion. When she was 16 and still waiting for her first pro event win, her father told *The New York Times*, "The only thing that can stop Venus from being Number One by eighteen is an accident."

And 1997 was the year Venus Williams would begin to prove that her father was onto something. That autumn, Venus played spectacularly well, reaching the finals of the U.S. Open, the first black woman to do so since Althea Gibson in 1958. Before the big event, regarded as the most important tournament in America, Venus had failed all attempts to reach the finals of the other pro events on her limited schedule. Yet, she continued to *act* like the champion she had been raised to believe she was, battling her opponents with an aggressive in-your-face style rarely seen in women's tennis.

39

"I Can Do This. I Know I Can."

At the U.S. Open, Venus's luck—and style—suddenly changed. "Something in her head finally clicked," Oracene noted. "How not to rush, how to play the game." Venus carefully slowed down her notoriously fast serve, and she began to mix her shots, learning from each game she played against the top-ranked women—and winning every match. This shift in style added to the mounting intimidation felt by her opponents. "We create it in our own heads: We're playing *Venus*!" admitted a surprised Jeanette Kruger, after losing out to the up-and-coming player. When Venus had suddenly grinned at her across the net, Kruger explained to the press, "It came over as, 'Do you have anything else to show me?'"

Such comments confused Venus, who responded upon hearing them, "When I want to smile, I'll smile. If I don't want to, I'm not going to. I think it's a little bit peevish. Smiling—what does that have to do with anything?"

What seemed to be of more importance to Venus was that with her U.S. Open debut, her world ranking jumped from 66th to a very respectable No. 26. Although she lost in the finals to Martina Hingis, a Czechoslovakian-born resident of Switzerland a few months younger than herself, Venus Williams's progress as a player was remarkable. Almost overnight, she had become a *force*, a tennis player everyone else fears. "Venus—holy mackerel! That's like a TV show," said the well-known tennis coach Nick Bollettieri.

Moving On Up

By September of 1997, Venus had earned $426,861 in prize money. Only 13 other female tennis players in the world had earned more that year. And Venus continued to play tennis, *great* tennis. "I think this year will probably be the most fun I'll ever have on the tour, watching my ranking progressively get better," Venus predicted.

Early in 1998, Venus won her first important tennis title in mixed doubles; that is, teamed up with a male player, in this case Justin Gimelstob. They won the title at the Australian Open, one of the sport's four big annual tournaments. These tournaments are referred to as "Grand Slam" events: the Australian Open held each January, the French Open in June, Wimbledon in June and July, and the U.S. Open in September.

The Australian Open was also special for Venus because it marked the first time she was able to play a professional match against younger sister Serena. The Williamses are the first black sisters to ever compete against each other in a pro event. "It wasn't fun eliminating my sister, but I have to be tough," Venus told reporters after Serena's loss. "After the match, I said, 'I'm sorry I had to take you out.'" Venus admitted, "Since I am older, I have the feeling I should win. I really wouldn't want to lose. But that's the only person I would be happy losing to because I would say, 'Go ahead, Serena. Go ahead, take the title.'"

Serena accepted her loss with dignity, hugging her sister at the end of the match. When the two clasped hands tightly, turned to the crowd, and bowed *together*, the applause was deafening. "If I had to lose . . . there's no one better to lose to than Venus," Serena said gracefully. Venus responded with equal diplomacy, "Serena hates to lose and her reputation is she

41

"I Can Do This. I Know I Can."

doesn't lose to anyone twice, so I'm going to be practicing secretly if I want to win the next one."

On March 1, 1998, Venus won again. This time she scored her first professional singles title in the IGA Tennis Classic in Oklahoma City. Almost a month later, Venus won her second big singles tournament title at the Lipton Championships in Key Biscayne. Also known in America as the fifth Grand Slam, the Lipton event was especially exciting for the Williams family because *both* of their rising stars got a shot at the reigning No. 1 player in women's

Playing against her sister Serena for the second time in mixed doubles, Venus shares the winners' trophy with partner Justin Gimelstob after their victory at the French Open in 1998.

tennis, Martina Hingis. Although her sister lost her match against the top player, Venus did not. "Serena gave me one pointer that really helped me." Venus told reporters. "'Go out and kick butt,'" Richard Williams claimed, "that was what [Serena] told her." Ranked No. 11, up 100 points from the previous year's Lipton, Venus defeated the No. 1 superstar in the semifinals and rose to the No. 10 slot.

Richard was generous in his excuses for Hingis's loss, as he would have been had it been his own daughter's. "The pressure of being Number One has drained the living hell out of Hingis. I've told Venus, 'Nineteen ninety-eight is your year to take the Number One spot.' But, as sad as this sounds, I kind of hope she doesn't take it this year. These girls, when they become Number One, they look older, they act older, they get tired fast. It's the pressure."

Venus was more blunt about her victory. "She isn't as strong as I am," she said of Hingis. "A lot of times the strong person doesn't have to think as much as the next person. When I learn to [think more], I'm going to become a much better player."

Richard, too, expects that Venus will improve markedly with full physical maturity. "Venus grew too fast," he remarked after her Lipton win. "She grew so fast, the muscle around her left knee hasn't filled in with the bone. When she hugged me after beating Hingis, she said, 'My knee is really hurting me, Daddy. I have to go see the trainer.'"

Her knee pain did not interfere with her sizzling serve, however, clocked at Lipton at 122 mph, the second fastest in the history of the women's tour. This speed topped by 12 mph the tournament's next fastest serve by a woman,

43

"I Can Do This. I Know I Can."

which happened to be hit by Serena. According to *Sports Illustrated*, of the 96 male players entered in the championships, an estimated 15 might have served faster than Venus. "I think she's the best athlete the women's game has seen so far," stated the famous tennis champion Andre Agassi, who lost in the Lipton men's final. "Now it's a matter of how she puts it all together. She's going to beat ninety-nine percent of the girls because of the athlete she is."

In the Lipton finals, Venus handily beat Anna Kournikova, the Russian 16-year-old who lives and trains in Miami Beach. Venus struggled at first, but quickly took control with what has been called her "powerhouse game." Kournikova, who was ranked 16th in the world at the time, blamed her own numerous mistakes for the loss, pointing sadly to all of her "unforced errors, I guess." Venus captured the $235,000 purse.

Grinning widely and holding up her Lipton Championships trophy, Venus posed proudly for photographers. Remembering her good manners, she waved Kournikova into the picture. Both girls, along with Martina Hingis and Serena, will probably remain in the big picture in the years to come. According to *Tennis* magazine, women's tennis is on the brink of a golden age because of this brilliant new generation of budding superstars. "It's a good sign for the future," Venus commented about the Florida women's tournament dominated by talented teens. "Everyone was exposed to the new girls."

Hard Courts

In May of 1998, Venus defeated Serena in their second meeting on the Women's Tennis

Association Tour, this time in the quarterfinals of the Italian Open. "I was a little disappointed," admitted Serena. "I went out there really wanting to win this time. But there will be another time."

Venus had her chance for disappointment next, losing the $150,000 prize to the tournament queen, her "old" nemesis, Martina Hingis. Their court meeting was labeled by the press as "the hottest rivalry in women's tennis." At the time, the No. 1 Hingis sported an impressive record of 30-3 for the year, with two of her only three losses going to Venus Williams. About her powerful challenger, Hingis admitted, "I was surprised at the way she played. She was fighting. She didn't give up until the end."

Venus, who is a much less experienced player, stands inches taller and plays more explosively. She proved to be an exciting opponent. "This was a new experience for me," the tenacious young tennis whiz acknowledged about her first-ever appearance in the prestigious clay court event. "In the end, [Hingis] played more aggressive. She decided to go for it and take more chances." Venus can be philosophical about her losses "Sometimes it's good to lose so you can learn. You learn more from when you lose than when you win."

The "new girls" soon convened again, this time in Paris for the '98 French Open, an even more important clay court tournament. In preparing for this next Grand Slam event, Venus and Serena skipped the sight-seeing to focus on practice. "We have no desires at this time—other than on the court," Venus said. By this time, Serena was ranked 27th in the world, and she awed both opponents and spectators with her strong returns and backhand winners, before losing to Arantxa Sanchez Vicario, a 26-year-old veteran player from Spain. Known to be a master of strategy, Vicario thrives against powerful hitters. "I taught her a lesson," bragged the older player, who accused Serena of disrespect. Serena commented dryly, "Every time I see her play a match, she always argues about almost every call. If she didn't do that, then I would have been a little surprised because she argues a lot."

Venus, by this time ranked No. 7 in the world, lost to arch rival Hingis in the quarterfinals in a swirling wind that tamed her strong serve. The match was sloppy, upset by gusts of wind and unforced errors, but Venus took the loss gracefully. "I think I didn't play as well as I should have," she admitted afterward. "I think [Hingis] played better. . . . She grew up on clay." Williams added in her own defense, "I grew up on hard courts."

The French Open women's trophy went to Sanchez Vicario, who beat another veteran, 24-year-old Monica Seles, in the final. Seles, who had trounced Hingis in the semifinals, might have deserved the sympathy vote more than Hingis or the Williams sisters did. Stabbed by a crazed fan on a tennis court in Germany in 1993, Seles had slowly recovered, only to begin nursing her father—and coach—until his death from cancer barely two weeks before the 1998 French Open began. Sanchez Vicario, who earned more than $600,000 for her victory, apologized to Seles: "I'm so sorry that I beat you. . . . I have a lot of respect for you, especially with all that happened. . . ."

A tearful Venus mourns her loss to Martina Hingis in the quarterfinal of the French Open in 1998. Although she had practiced hard, Venus could not overcome Hingis's aggressive playing.

5

COURTING SUCCESS

"I'm sure if Venus had played more, she would have been even better than she is sooner," Martina Hingis told *GQ* in June 1998. Pam Shriver, who was a U.S. Open finalist when she was only 16, recently told *People*, "Most champions or potential champions have this special attitude that sets them apart. Sometimes it comes across as arrogance." Other, less gracious, players have complained about Venus Williams, claiming that she doesn't play enough, that she is too distant, arrogant, and unfriendly. Seles informed the press, "I said once to Venus, 'Hi,' and she didn't say it back. She seems to be going all the time with her sister, her mom, too." But Seles understands making such choices in the dangerous world of women's professional tennis. "That's what family is for. They stay in their own little separate group."

Venus and Serena, who braid and bead each other's hair and consider themselves best friends, illustrated this point the time they were spotted in the hallway of the Arthur Ashe Stadium, their arms locked, their beads clattering, singing and dancing as they walked. "I'm looking to win matches, to be the best. I'm not looking for friends.

Ranked 66th at the U.S. Open in 1997, Venus defeated 11th-seeded Irina Spirlea of Rumania in the women's semifinals, enabling Venus to go on to the finals against Martina Hingis.

You really can't find a friend these days. You have your family, you have your God, and that's about it," Venus summarized in response to the accusations that she goes her own way. "I don't see why anyone should be upset that I'm close to my family, because a lot of people don't even have that."

Richard, too, has landed in the midst of controversy a number of times, usually after making uncensored statements to the media. For example, Richard announced just before the 1997 U.S. Open final—played for the first time in the new stadium in Flushing Meadow, New York, named for the African-American tennis legend Arthur Ashe—that both he and Venus had heard players use the word "nigger." When white reporters at Venus's next press conference attempted to elicit a response from her to her father's statement, one black reporter left the room in protest. Venus collected herself and said, "I think with this moment in the first year in Arthur Ashe Stadium, it all represents everyone being together, everyone having a chance to play. So I think this is definitely ruining the mood, these questions about racism."

Despite all of the media fuss, tennis fans worship Venus. She in turn loves to sign autographs for fans, especially the children. "Oh, my God," shrieked a young fan toting a tournament poster after spotting Venus at a mall. "The beads are even awesomer in real life." Richard declares, "I have never seen a girl that the public takes to as much as they do Venus. She reminds me of Ali," he says, referring to the popular boxer and media favorite Muhammad Ali.

In 1997, while on a 10-day trip to Russia to play in the Ladies Kremlin Cup, Venus kept an

on-line diary for the Women's Tennis Association website, sharing her unique experiences and refreshingly youthful views with her many fans.

"I have seen a lot of Russia. The place is replete with history that is very interesting. The art here is wonderful also, and the people are very talented. It is great that they are finally being given the chance to live a more free life, with the fall of Communism. Okay, that's enough of that."

Whenever she faces the media, Venus outshines all but the most sophisticated

Although some players have criticized Venus as often aloof, the young star's fans don't seem to share that attitude, as one demonstrated with a hug at the 1998 Australian Open.

Venus, who thoroughly enjoys her popularity with her fans, doesn't hesitate to sign autographs, as she is doing here after an appearance on David Letterman's show in 1998.

superstars. She is relaxed and poised, smart and spunky, always wearing up-to-the-minute fashions and ever ready with an intelligent comment or bright sound-bite. "That question does not compute," she will tease an overly intrusive interviewer. She has appeared on *The Late Show with David Letterman*, and has been featured on *60 Minutes*. On the air with Jay Leno in 1998, Venus wowed the audience with her tiny, black slip dress, and she managed to get lots of laughs at the expense of her host. "You've got the P.R. game down," Leno whistled. "Whoa. You're gonna be huge."

Venus is also comfortable in her public role as a fashion icon on and off the court, modeling the retro-cool look with her powder-blue leather jacket, baggy bell-bottom blue jeans, and sweaters in bright colors like mint and peach, accentuated with gold and silver necklaces, rings, and two watches. "That's just the way I am. I have a lot of clothes and a lot of jewelry," Venus laughs.

Oracene, who also wears beaded braids, attributes her daughter's cool, calm demeanor while in the public eye to her special upbringing. Both Venus and Serena were "encouraged to be themselves, not to have any inhibitions," their mother explains. "You're not really having fun if you're not being yourself."

Slice Girls

Except for her multimillion-dollar earnings and worldwide celebrity status, Venus Williams seems to be a pretty regular teenager who manages to have quite a bit of fun. Relatively unfazed by her personal success, Venus wants to have more than a tennis career in her life.

After graduating with a 3.8 average from high school, Venus began taking classes at Palm Beach Community College when she was 17. She still lives at home. "My parents were taught that family should be together, and that's how they taught us," Venus says. "I definitely don't plan to move away from my family. I'll probably live in the lot next door."

Venus has talked of opening a young people's clothing store in the Palm Beach area (with Mom and Serena) and has mentioned the possibility of studying archaeology or anthropology. She currently takes college courses as her tennis schedule permits but intends to end her tennis career by the time she is 26. Then she may become a clothing designer or an architect—or both. "I have the potential," Venus says, confident as always in her future and her own abilities.

Venus likes to listen to alternative rock music, and she and Serena prefer the newer bands popular with Generation Xers, like Rancid, Hole, Green Day, and Bad Religion. She plays guitar and enjoys strumming her reissued 1957 Fender Stratocaster. "I used to play air guitar on my tennis racket a lot, so I decided to learn," she explains. Venus also likes roller-blading on the smooth Palm Beach sidewalks and surfing with Serena off the Florida coast. (Serena reports, "I had a rotten, ugly, horrible, nasty, funky boogie board. I got a short board so I could rip and shred, but Venus went crazy and got a ten-footer.") And, oh yes, Venus *loves* shopping. "At one time I would just buy, buy, buy," Venus admits sheepishly. Now, she plans ahead for what she will shop for, "so I don't go crazy."

At a promotional event held a few days before one of the girls' pro tennis tournaments, the sisters played a version of *Supermarket Sweep*, their favorite television show. Piling products into their shopping carts, Venus and Serena were in teen heaven. "It's like realizing a dream," said the enthralled Venus. "I always wanted to be on that show." Serena added, "I can't stop thinking about it. I could do this, like, every day." Richard commented with a smile, "This makes up for all the days when we didn't have enough money to spend at the grocery store. They were probably having flashbacks."

The Williams sisters eat typical teen fast-food favorites—tacos, chicken nuggets, chili dogs—and talk a lot about typical teen topics, mostly jewelry, clothes, and of course, boys. "Reggie Miller [a basketball player] came to a match I played. The only thing was, I didn't even know he was there," Venus once admitted to a reporter. "My mom told me that she'd seen him there three days *later.* And she didn't even tell him I wanted to meet him. I mean, what was she thinking? I was like, 'Mom, you should have *said* something.'" Venus is currently enamored with Kobe Bryant, a guard for the Los Angeles Lakers, because, "he really inspires me. He plays professional basketball, he's going to be the next Michael Jordan, he still takes classes at UCLA, and he speaks Italian fluently." Turning to Serena, Venus quips, "And what are you doing?" "I speak fluent Ebonics and English. I am currently in high school, and I have read *Hamlet,*" recites Serena. Oracene rolls her eyes and the girls laugh. They definitely love to have fun.

Dubbed "The Sunglass Girls" by the almost totally white crowd at the '97 Australian Open, Venus and Serena were treated like Michael Jordan themselves, becoming the focus of public attention, lots of television cameras, and much media hype. The girls had a blast cavorting in their designer shades and collecting "units" from Mom, who passed out money for food in the players' cafeteria and at the hotel. With a friend, a junior player from California, Venus and Serena devised their own Top 10 list of men on the tour, a list which combines tennis talent with, of course, physical appearance. Who is their No. 1 guy? "Ohhhh, Pete," Serena gushes, meaning Pete Sampras, the hunky 26-year-old American men's champ.

When Richard heard that it would cost more than $29,000 for the family to fly to Australia business class, he decided to stay home. Oracene and the girls traveled coach for slightly more than $6,000. Richard does not like to fly anyway, so Oracene usually takes his place on the overseas tour stops. There is no entourage, and Oracene serves as hairdresser as well as substitute coach when they travel. She says of their practice of traveling in the coach section of airplanes, "I'm not going to pay all of that money. I feel like I'm cheating somebody who needs it." Venus counters, "In first class, everybody has their business papers and stuff. If you could lean over you could probably learn to make some money. In second class, if you don't watch out, they'll steal your wallet." Mom picks up the strands of a very worn argument. "If it were up to me, Venus wouldn't even have a car." Venus jokes back, "If it were up to you, we'd all be eating rice and barley." The girls snicker.

Doing It Their Own Way

Unlike most of the superstars who are her peers in attaining early fame and fortune, Venus, the young tennis champ and sports celebrity, has a refreshingly down-to-earth lifestyle. The family lives in a modest-sized house on an estate, where Venus enjoys playing competitive video games with her father and horsing around with her sister, who is younger "by one year, three months, and nine days," says the sometimes composed, sometimes giggly Venus. The two girls love to pose for each other, mugging and chuckling while snapping pictures with Venus's tiny Pentax camera. "They never stop," says Oracene. The sisters zip around their rural compound in golf carts, bike-dive into one of the two lakes on their spacious property—dubbed "Lake Superior" and "Lake Inferior"—and practice their killer serves on a red hard court emblazoned with "Williams" in huge white letters across a green backdrop.

In preparing for a pro event, the sisters practice a lot, talk to reporters a little, and spend much time together. They usually coordinate the color schemes for their beaded hairdos in advance, and may discuss eye color as well, using nonprescription contact lenses to change their brown eyes to blue, gray, green, or lilac. The beads were actually Oracene's idea, to create a hairstyle that is easy to care for. It takes 90 minutes to braid in the beads, but the hairdo looks great for five or six weeks since they can wash their hair without removing the beads.

There is no personal trainer, masseuse, or high-tech weight room at home. A fit 169 pounds, Venus does not adhere to any formal road conditioning or weight-lifting program. In fact, when she was 15, Venus would race her three dogs in order to keep fit for tennis. "I give myself a head start, and then they chase after me. They beat me—they're really fast," she laughed when describing her unique "training program" with a Dalmatian and two mutts. (The girls were crushed recently when one of their dogs, Princess, drowned in "Lake Superior." But now they have a new puppy appropriately named Star.) At the '98 French Open, Serena's unorthodox tennis tunic bared her strong back

Venus (right) and Serena pair up for a doubles match at the Italian Open in May 1998. As a doubles team, Venus and Serena are still unranked, but that is likely to change as they compete in more events together.

muscles, contributing to the mystique about her powerful physique. Serena, like Venus, does not work out with weights.

Although she is, at five feet ten, nearly four inches shorter than her sister, Serena is a more muscular 145 pounds. Her favorite tennis outfits—designed with T-backs and no sleeves—accentuate her impressive build. "I guess it looks like I have a lot of muscles here," she joked with reporters after intimidating opponents on the French clay courts. "I mean, my arms are just naturally like this. I hate lifting weights. I just hate doing that stuff. It's too much." Good-natured as always, Serena flexed her rippling back muscles for the curious reporters, then laughed.

Even though Serena recently signed an endorsement deal with Puma, Richard Williams sometimes threatens to pull Serena off the tennis courts and send her to a college campus instead because, he worries, "She's too bright." She reads the classics while waiting in the stands during pro tennis matches (she polished off Charles Dickens's *A Tale of Two Cities* at 1997's Wimbledon) and plans on becoming a veterinarian.

When Venus was in New York making world history at the '97 U.S. Open, Richard told *Ebony* magazine that he wished his daughter would "get the hell out of New York and get back to pursuing [her] education. I would like to see her get out of tennis completely. She has proven to the world what she can do. I would like to see her get out before she gets hooked. It's very difficult when people are offering you all this money," the concerned dad complained. "Education is power, not chasing around some ball." Even though his girls are undisputed superathletes, Richard continues to air his mixed feelings about the impact of a pro tennis career on his two teenaged daughters. "It's not important anymore for them to be good players. It used to be. No more. What I want is for them to be good human beings," he has said.

When Boris Becker was only 17 years old, he became the youngest man in history to win Wimbledon. A decade later, after years of impressing his opponents and wowing his fans, Becker decided to retire. "I'm glad I made it out alive, to tell you the truth," Becker admits. "I was always praying that I somehow would have a long career, and I managed to do that without any major scars in my soul. I'm not drug addicted, I'm not alcoholic, I'm not three times divorced. I'm quite normal. I manage to have a quite normal life. For me, that was always my biggest achievement."

This is the challenge for the *new* first family of tennis: Venus Williams, her sister Serena, and their parents. They have already managed to move from the Los Angeles ghetto to a spectacular spread in Palm Beach Gardens, Florida. The girls have both been able to beat some of the highest-ranking tennis players on the professional women's circuit. Venus has college courses under her belt, Serena is still in school. The two teens face their audiences and the press with dignity and good humor. They love one another, the family is very tight, their priorities are in order.

The Williams family appears to be handling their unique situation very successfully, as Venus—and, perhaps, Serena as well—follow in the historic footsteps of the African-American tennis legends Arthur Ashe and Althea Gibson. The Williamses are forging ahead and they are doing it *their* way. "We couldn't care less what people think of us," Richard Williams once told *Sports Illustrated* after some heated commentary in the press. What the Williams family does care about is one another, doing what is right for them, and doing their best. "What's good for us is what we know," states Oracene, "because we run this family."

"I sit back and I watch my daughters and I feel like I've done a great job with them," Richard said recently. "My girls are obedient, responsible, and they know commitment. . . . Everything I've done so far, I think I've done the right thing. My girls have an education."

The girls agree. "He's somewhat of a genius at

what he does," Venus offers. "He's more than a genius," adds Serena. "Sometimes I think he is Superman."

To the Top

"She's in a great position, and she's been raised to be in that position as an African American in a mostly white sport," says Zina Garrison of Venus Williams. Garrison, a fellow black female tennis pro, played on the women's tour herself for more than 15 years. "It helps her that she has the strength, confidence, and arrogance you need to become the top player in the world. I see her going straight to the top."

To say that her climb in the world tennis rankings has been meteoric is an understatement. At the start of 1997, Venus ranked 211th, and her total earnings amounted to less than $32,000. By June of 1998, she ranked 7th and had brought home more than half-a-million dollars in purse money that year alone.

Although sometimes rivals on the court, as they were at the Australian Open, Venus (right) and Serena, shown here with Oracene at that event, are devoted companions off the court. They practice together and love each other's company whether on shopping sprees, having fun, or just "horsing around."

Venus gives the game every ounce of herself in a return shot during a doubles match at the Evert Cup in March 1997. The Evert Cup presented Venus with her first big prize money and firmly established her reputation as a major competitor in the world of women's tennis.

Recently labeled by the Associated Press as "one of the hottest properties in women's tennis," Venus continues her speed-of-light rise. Her star is shining *very* brightly these days.

"Here comes the Wimbledon trophy," yells Richard to a smiling Venus after she drives a strong serve deep into her (older, male) practice partner's court. "Let me hold the purse." (The prize money for the 1998 women's singles title was nearly $650,000.) Venus does a little dance, then she gets ready to hit the ball again, *hard*. She stares straight ahead, her large almond-shaped eyes on the Wimbledon purse, the world's top spot in women's professional tennis, and beyond.

CAREER TOURNAMENT STATS

(Adapted from COREL WTA TOUR Media Information System)

YEAR	DATE	EVENT	PRIZE	TOTAL WINS/LOSSES	RANK
1994	November 6	Oakland	$ 5,350	1/1	0
1995	August 13	Los Angeles	$ 1,295	0/1	0
	August 20	Canadian Open	$ 2,175	0/2	0
	November 5	Oakland	$ 10,215	2/3	321
1996	March 17	Indian Wells	$ 1,500	0/1	217
	April 14	Amelia Island	$ 1,285	2/2	197
	August 18	Los Angeles	$ 4,215	4/3	192
	August 25	San Diego	$ 2,600	4/4	148
	November 10	Oakland	$ 3,150	7/5	207
1997	March 16	Indian Wells	$ 20,500	3/1	211
	March 30	Lipton	$ 6,750	7/2	110
	April 13	Amelia Island	$ 2,150	8/3	102
	June 8	French Open	$ 14,520	11/4	90
	June 22	Eastbourne	$ 4,950	12/5	79
	July 6	Wimbledon	$ 7,701	15/6	59
	August 3	San Diego	$ 4,950	16/7	64
	August 10	Los Angeles	$ 4,950	20/8	59
	August 17	DuMaurier Open (Toronto)	$ 2,650	20/9	53
	September 7	U.S. Open	$ 350,000	26/10	66
	October 12	Filderstadt (Germany)	$ 675	26/11	26
	October 19	Zurich (Switzerland)	$ 16,875	27/12	26
	November 2	Moscow (Russia)	$ 16,875	32/13	24
	November 16	Philadelphia	$ 2,600	32/14	25
1998	January 18	Sydney (Australia)	$ 26,500	4/1	21
	February 1	Australian Open	$ 55,667	8/2	16
	March 1	Oklahoma City	$ 27,000	13/2	14
	March 15	Indian Wells	$ 41,750	16/3	12
	March 29	Lipton	$ 235,000	22/3	11
	May 10	Italian Open (Rome)	$ 60,000	27/4	9
	June 7	French Open (Paris)	$ 75,700	31/5	7
	September 9	U.S. Open	$ 200,000	39/9	5

61

CHRONOLOGY

1980   Venus Ebone Starr Williams is born on June 17 in Lynwood, California.

1984   Begins playing tennis on neighborhood courts in Compton, California, with father Richard Williams as coach/manager.

1990   Unbeaten in junior tennis circuit; scouted by Florida coach Rick Macci.

1991   Enrolls in Rick Macci's tennis program at the International Tennis Academy; Macci serves as coach (until 1995).

1994   Turns pro, playing limited schedule.

1995   Reebok offers $12-million endorsement deal; Williams family relocates to Palm Beach Gardens estate; Richard Williams resumes role as coach.

1996   Reebok debuts "The Venus Williams Collection" sportswear line.

1997   Graduates from high school and begins taking courses at area community college; first black woman since Althea Gibson in 1958 to reach finals of U.S. Open; year's prize money totals almost $470,000.

1998   Wins first professional event, mixed doubles at Australian Open; plays sister Serena in first professional event; wins first professional singles title at IGA Classic; first American-born woman to win Lipton Championships in 12 years; reaches No. 5 in women's world tennis rankings.

FURTHER READING

Collins, Bud and Zender Hollander, Editors. *Bud Collins' Tennis Encyclopedia*. Detroit: Visible Ink Press, 1997.

Davidson, Owen and C.M. Jones. *Great Women Tennis Players*. London: Pelham Books, 1971.

Gibson, Althea. *I Always Wanted To Be Somebody*. New York: Harper & Brothers, 1958.

Johnson, Anne Janette. *Great Women in Sports*. Detroit: Visible Ink Press, 1996.

King, Billie Jean and Cynthia Starr. *We Have Come a Long Way: The Story of Women's Tennis*. New York: McGraw Hill Book Company, 1988.

Mewshaw, Michael. *Ladies of the Court*. New York: Crown Publishers, 1993.

Neill, Michael. "Venus Rising," *People*, October 27, 1997.

Nelson, Jill. "The New First Family of Tennis," *USA Weekend*, April 10-12, 1998.

Teitelbaum, Michael. *Grand Slam Stars Martina Hingis and Venus Williams*. New York: Harper Active, 1998.

ABOUT THE AUTHOR

Virginia Aronson is the author of 14 books, including texts and how-to guides on health and fitness. She also writes books for young people as well as poetry and plays. Aronson lives in south Florida with her writer husband and their young son.

INDEX

PHOTO CREDITS:
AP/Wide World Photos: 2, 6, 9, 11, 12, 15, 19, 22, 24, 28, 31, 32, 34, 36, 38, 41, 45, 46, 49, 56, 59, 60; Library of Congress/Corbis: 17; Photofest: 50.